I0191472

Fragments Of A Quiet
Life

Nupur Gupta

BookLeaf
Publishing

India | USA | UK

Made with ❤ on the BookLeaf Publishing Platform
www.bookleafpub.in
www.bookleafpub.com

Dedication

To my sister -
the best cheerleader one could ask for!

Preface

This collection is a quiet offering.
It is made of soft mornings and long-held silences, of the small, ordinary moments that often go unnoticed—warm sheets, tea steam, the hush between conversations. These poems are not declarations, but observations. They do not chase joy, but sit beside it, learning how it comes and goes without asking for permission.

In a world that rewards noise and speed, these poems seek stillness. They try to name the feelings that don't announce themselves loudly—grief that lingers softly, happiness that arrives uninvited, peace that feels like coming home.

If you've ever felt too much over too little, or found comfort in the gentlest places, this book is for you. May you find something familiar here. May it remind you that nothing ordinary is ever truly small.

Acknowledgements

Like the contents of this book, I will keep this short and simple: there are four people in my life, who have always seen the potential in my writing and encouraged me to practice it when I was too afraid to even try. My sweet sister Sonal, my dear friends Rajul & Komal, and my loving husband, Sarang. This book could not have happened without your belief in me.

Nature's hope

The sky remembered something I forgot
But when I looked out my window today
Catching a break from the mid-evening fray
There it was again, suspended in thought

Between the pink, orange and golden hues
On top of the city's building snouts
As the sun fell on the autumn clouds
It cleared the cobwebs of my memory too

And I was back again,
on the roof of my childhood house
Standing next to my sister, mother and father
Looking at the sun set, behind the clouds

Admiring the beauty of nature
In one of its purest of forms
Was one of the reprieves we had normed
When the world was suspended mid fracture

As the agents of death sprouted wings
Forcing everyone to move within
Little families across the globe
Rediscovered solace inside their homes

And I hope I never forget that again
That we found light
even on the darkest of days
Because we always had each other

"Are you there?"

A quiet enquiry, sent at 3
three simple words that seem to be
On the face of it, a bit incomplete
But condense all the hurt of a burn of third degree

A cry for help,
from the heart swells
to reach out to the kindred spirit
at the other end of the cell

the screen lights up
the words appear
"Are you there?"
"yes, I'm here"
always, right here

Lullaby

I lie awake in bed
As you whisper lullabies of woodland creatures
My sister is already fed
Deep sleep evident in her features

But I hold on until the end
Hoping the characters don't run in a dead end

Little did I know
That those were the jewels
That you were imparting
From your half forgotten youth

And now you are gone
But life still goes on
And I try to find traces of you
In everyday rituals that I try to hold on to

But I'm afraid I'll end up forgetting you
Maybe, if there's hope in this world,

We will meet again
Maybe, in a lullaby

Flimsy dreams

Once a brand new notebook
now just crumbing letters
hiding for a long time in the nook
now my dreams fly away on its feathers

bubbling with hope you had been
when I first bought you on a whim
since then daylight you've hardly seen
as daily tasks made inspiration dim

days grow long
and life grows short
The mystery of the heart's song
never could be sought

so stay as you will, upon that sill
and keep making my heart want to spill

The Moonflower

Midnight glooms
Often bloom
When you are not there
In this room

An hour away
But a world apart
Distance did not care
What was in the heart

Each time we met
The clock would reset
And deepen the tear
in the scar

Bittersweet is this fate
which continues to cling
But sweetest yet
is the hope you bring

It's okay

It's okay
If some days you want to sleep in rather than face the
tiring world

It's okay
if some days instead of braving crowds at the local
market you'd rather be on your couch, curled

It's okay
If sometimes you say no to your friends and instead
danced in your room and twirled

And it's always okay
To choose yourself, over and over again, until the last
shred of insecurity in your heart has unfurled

The heartbreak of entangled dreams

While people my age
Were dealing with heartbreaks
I struggled for my goals

I bled sweat, as they shed tears
Rooting for my future self
While they yearned for other souls

Bated breath

Time stops
and the world holds its breath
as we each hold on to our loved ones
praying to not make that list of death

Empty promises and sweet nothings
fill the space between the four walls
As we each try to hold on to our sanity
and not let our small universe fall

but words run out
and so does the patience
and the only thing keeping us in,
is the will to not become the next patient

So hold on for a while longer
because nothing lasts forever
this too shall come to pass
because time stops for no one, ever

Shades of Grey

When we are little
Everything is black and white
There's always a villain
That gets slain by the knight

But as we grow up
The colors start to get messy
Not all villains are that bad
Nor all heroes that brawny

But the biggest change
Comes on the day
When we learn to look within
And find all shades of grey

Guilty pleasure

Sunday afternoons
Soft light filtering through the rooms
A sense of magical realism in the air
Like endless possibilities are finally within stare

Heart full of moons
Soul singing with the tunes
I can finally let go of the pressure
As I indulge in some guilty pleasure

What is life?

Having always wondered what the meaning of life was
The best explanation that I have been able to come up
with is this: it is the beautiful act of understanding...

Perhaps the entire point in us being here is to
understand
Our parents, our brothers and our sisters
Our teachers, our bosses, and our friends

The birds and the trees
The mountains and the oceans
Why our stomach does that weird dip when the airplane
takes off
Why there must be a dawn before the sun comes up

But most of all, this life seems to be
a lifelong experiment in understanding,
above all and beyond,
Ourselves

Inherited dreams

I want to write,
but I don't know what
feelings seek freedom
I know not from what

An outlet they seek
my pen my only medium,
but words elude me
leaving me forever reeling...

A cup of coffee
a flat table top
the quiet of the noon
and the soul that was not

meant to be content
in this world of inheritance
but what are we receiving, if not
broken hopes, shattered dreams, baseless fears
a broken heart.

The Truth

Truth wears a mask
That changes with light
And when things begin to turn dark
It gets ready to flight

A tool to one
And a prayer for another
The shapes and forms it can don
Leaves room for some terror

And yet it remains
the sneakiest creature out there
For truth always claws its way back
No matter the depth of the snare

City where rain falls upwards

Everything slowed down
And time lost its anchor
While rain poured all around
We huddled closer to our platters

The raging cloudburst had been
An unexpected adversary
Drowning out the well laid plans
In which you had poured your energy

The long winding walks
Littered with several cozy pitstops
As well as that old banyan tree
Were all left wanting, covered in dewdrops

And though fret you did
Wanting rain to fall upwards
I would never change any moment of that day
When I fell for you a little further

Introspection

I am afraid of the page
Of what I will find
When I open the drawers
Of my mind

Midnight red and sparkly blues
but regret comes to me
Only in grey hues

But it matters not
The size of the ghosts
If we choose only to look
At all the golden zones

Expectations

People say it's better to not have
any expectations
of people and projects
dreams and work

But if we have
no expectations, no hope,
no dreams, no goals
nothing to aspire to
or desire or want

are we even alive?
Isn't that what life is?
To look forward to things

to eagerly await for the next chapter in our story?
What the next day, next month, next year brings?

At its core
It's the small hope

of a better, more exciting tomorrow
that keeps us going forth

So the next time you are asked
to keep your expectations in check
remind yourself of what it means
to be alive in this deck

Stolen time

Forgotten laptops
Unanswered texts
Everything seemed suspended
Holding its breath

As the soft afternoon sun filtered
through the steam rising from the pasta pot
And the soft tunes of piano
Occupied a corner of the house

We leaned a little closer
Hands brushing and lingering for longer
It was a time outside of time
Something we borrowed from our busy lives

Reflections of Self

Some days I wake up
Feeling like someone else
Like the real me was the one
That got left behind in a cell

A hazy tint
Clouds over the mind
And though the body is here
The heart is in a bind

Nothing makes me feel
An ounce of energy
There is neither anger nor sadness
Behind this lethargy

Just as surreptitiously
As this other self arrives
So too it departs some days
Without leaving any memory behind

Rejuvenation

Stillness holds a seed
Softly, the earth begins to breathe
And I rise with the green
As it pushes through the creek

Wind's fury

The day I stopped running, the wind finally spoke to me.
What started as a whisper, quickly turned into a gale,
forcing me to face the truths, of the half-realities I had
forged in my brain.

The various insecurities, the cobwebs of my
shortcomings, were all blown away, as the wind cleared
the path to the only actuality.

There is no lack. No glass to fill or measure. For each
soul is complete on its own when it reaches this pasture,
we just need to ensure we appreciate it in its own
personality.

Finding Joy

People spend decades
Trying to find happiness in their lives
But what always fascinates me
Is how ordinarily joy arrives

It nestles softly
In the scent of clean sheets
Warm toasts and a cup of tea
bring solace to all lost fleets

Whether on the top of a mountain
Or the bottom of a river bed
Joy can spring forth like a fountain
As long as we keep our hearts clear

www.ingramcontent.com/pod-product-compliance
Lightning Source LLC
Chambersburg PA
CBHW051001030426
42339CB00007B/432